ANXIETY

*Overcome Anxiety Permanently
Without Medication*

By Gerard Johnson

TABLE OF CONTENTS

Lavender (No Drowse)

Chamomile

Passion Flower

Lemon Balm

Ashwagandha

Hops

Green Tea

Chapter 5 - Let's Talk and Socialize

Chapter 6 - The Benefits of Exercise in Anxiety

Wait. How Do Exercise Exactly Work in Anxiety?

Simple and Really Quick Exercises and Tips

Chapter 7 - How Music Affects Your Brain

Chapter 8 - Relaxation Techniques to Battle Anxiety

Conclusion

Legal & Disclaimer

Legal & Disclaimer

The information contained in this book is not designed to replace or take the place of any form of medicine or professional medical advice. The information in this book has been provided for educational and entertainment purposes only.

The information contained in this book has been compiled from sources deemed reliable, and it is accurate to the best of the Author's knowledge; however, the Author cannot guarantee its accuracy and validity and cannot be held liable for any errors or omissions. Changes are periodically made to this book. You must consult your doctor or get

Introduction

Do you feel too unsettled and have you spent the rest of your night tossing and turning in your bed because you can't sleep? Do you worry too much? Are you feeling exceptionally stressed and rattled lately? Is it already dragging for days, weeks or months? Is it hindering you from functioning properly and being normally productive? If yes, then I am afraid you are suffering from anxiety disorder.

You see, there is nothing wrong with being anxious. Everyone gets anxious at some point in their lives, especially before big events. However, if you are almost always anxious and it drags for days and practically affects your daily living, that is already considered a disorder.

Okay, so you have a disorder, but you don't want it treated with medicines. What can you do?

In this book, we will discuss further what anxiety disorder is, where it came from and we will also identify its signs and symptoms. I have also dedicated an entire chapter to discuss the truth that pharmaceutical companies don't tell you about synthetic medicines. With that in mind, I have also made a side-by-side comparison of natural remedies and synthetic medicines to help you find out their differences and let you know the benefits of natural remedies.

Those chapters will be followed by the different types of remedies with some tips and step-by-step instructions that you can opt for instead of stuffing yourself with medications that do not only cost too much but may also cost you your overall health and even life. We have natural medications like herbs and teas, we have relaxation techniques, exercises, music, and socialization. Dig in and have fun!

Thank you for downloading this book.

Chapter 1

What is Anxiety?

Many people use the word anxiety freely. Some people know the real meaning of it and some just say it just because they keep hearing it from other people. But what really is anxiety, anyway?

Anxiety is a strong emotion that is characterized by worrying, nervousness, and being uneasy because of something that is uncertain. How easy it is to define in words, but if you are the one experiencing the anxiety, it's not as easy. However, you have to understand that just because you are experiencing anxiety, it doesn't mean that you are already suffering from a disorder.

The strong emotion called anxiety is actually related to humanity's *fight or flight* response meaning it is perfectly normal for a person to feel agitated, nervous, worried or even experience the difficulty of sleeping especially the day before a big event is to happen.

What is "Fight or Flight" Response?

We always hear the words "fight or flight" response whenever a number of psychological disorders are being discussed. Many people know its meaning, but only a few know how deep this response covers. Before we proceed, let me tell you about it.

It all traces back when man still roamed the surface of the Earth endlessly to hunt for food and find a safe place to live. Our ancestors, being exposed in a life of endless running and endless hunting just to survive, developed the fight or flight response.

It is the body's response whenever we feel threatened or if a dangerous situation is about to happen. Whenever our ancestors feel threatened, their bodies release several hormones like *cortisol* and even *adrenaline* to help us prepare ourselves physically in case the situation requires us to fight or run.

The hormones that our body releases are meant to keep us physically, yet temporarily, well-equipped like making our hearts beat faster for better blood circulation that will concentrate on the parts of our bodies that need it the most. These hormones also keep us even more conscious to what is happening to our surroundings.

Once the threatening situation is out of the way, or bodies start to relax by releasing hormones that encourage muscle relaxation. If you have experienced *adrenaline rush* you must have also felt how your whole body shook after the adventure. That normally happens as the body is relaxing the muscles.

Anxiety only becomes a disorder once it starts to take over your entire life. Ever recall being so alarmed, bothered, and you can't get settled for days or weeks just because of one normal thing like going out of the house on your own? Think and try to remember any instance.

You see, it is okay and very normal to feel anxious about something that is new or unusual to you, but if your reason to get anxious is things that one can do regularly and normally in life, then you might very well be already suffering from anxiety disorder.

Some example of experiences of people with anxiety disorders are:

- Marcus cannot get settled with his door with just one lock. It has been bothering him for a few days and only got contented after having two other locks installed on his door.

- Marcus always sees to it that the windows are shut and all the doors are locked before he opens his wallet or any kind of envelope for fear of having someone attack him because of money.

- Sandrine cannot leave the house on her own because she is afraid she might get lost. She waits for her husband to get home or fetch her just so she can leave the house.

The Signs and Symptoms of Anxiety Disorder

Just like any other disorder and even illness, anxiety disorder comes with signs and symptoms. It is imperative that you learn about this so you can evaluate yourself properly. In case you find yourself thinking over and over because of many matches you got from the list below, don't hesitate to consult a doctor for it. There's no harm in doing so. Anyway, let us continue below.

Chronic Indigestion – Continuously feeling bloated, constipation and some other difficulty that involves your digestive track.

Cold Hands and Feet – Cold extremities due to nervousness or feeling dizzy and nauseous.

Compulsive Behavior – Unexplained and excessive compulsion. Usually related to Obsessive Compulsive Disorder (OCD) which is considered a type of anxiety disorder.

Dizziness – Related to feeling nauseous, nervous, and fearful.

Dry Mouth – Commonly related to feeling nauseous, nervous, and fearful.

Excessive Worry – The kind of worry that lasts for days, even months, and usually hinders you from getting proper sleep.

Fidgety – Related to excessive worry.

Flashbacks – Related to excessive worry and phobia. Also known as Post-traumatic stress disorder or PTSD which is considered to be a type of anxiety disorder, just like perfectionism and OCD.

Irrational Fears – The kind of fear that keeps you from functioning properly to do every day normal stuff. This is a definite sign that someone is suffering from a phobia.

Lack of Sleep – Commonly related to excessive worry for unknown reasons and irrational fears. Not always, but can be a sign of anxiety especially if chronic.

Muscle Tension – Related to irrational fear.

Nausea – Related to irrational fear and lack of sleep.

Palpitation – Commonly related to irrational fear.

Panic – Panic is almost always accompanied by difficulty in breathing, sweating, dizziness, palpitations, numbness or tingling of the feet and hands, weakness, chest and stomach pain and feeling cold or hot all over. Commonly related to irrational fear and excessive worry. It is also important to remember that not everyone who experiences panic attack is suffering from anxiety disorder.

Perfectionism – A chronic habit that requires everything to be arranged and organized properly. This hinders an individual from being functional and productive. Perfectionism is also considered to be a type of anxiety disorder.

Self-Consciousness – Commonly related to excessive worry.

Self-Doubt – Self-doubt can be alarming if the unanswered question that bothers you become an obsession. Commonly related to perfectionism.

Social Anxiety Disorder – Commonly related to excessive worry. Somewhat similar to shyness, but just like any other disorder, it stops you from functioning as a normal human being in a society. The common option of people suffering from this to leave or avoid situations where they will encounter a big number of people.

Chapter 2

The Unspoken Truth About Prescribed and Over-the-Counter Medications and Supplements

What's the deal with the commonly known drug anyway? Why opt for natural medications than these "well-researched" ones?

Back when I was a kid, all I knew was that whenever I felt bad, my mom and some medicine will sort everything out. Those medicines tasted unpleasant, but they worked like magic. I thought of medicines that way until recently, I heard a news regarding an acquaintance of mine. He's now scheduled to have two sessions of dialysis every week. And the reason? Excessive intake of paracetamol.

While most of us resort to drugs to treat our illnesses, it is important for you to know that drugs can also cause diseases due to a number of reasons like adverse reactions and even the ingredients used for it and its coating. Now, you might wonder how it all happened so I decided to enumerate a couple of things below to help you find the truth about over-the-counter and prescribed medications.

- **Drugs and Supplements with Coating**

Drug and supplements that are coated especially the ones with time-releasing properties aren't exactly as good as you think. The coatings of some of those drugs contain potentially harmful chemicals including *phthalates*. Yes, I just stressed that word so you can remember it well because we will discuss that in one of the bullets below.

For the meantime, whenever purchasing some over-the-counter drugs or even the prescribed ones, take good care in reading the labels and its ingredients. Actually, you might want to pay more attention to reading the *inactive ingredients* because you might just encounter **phthalates** there. In cases where inactive ingredients or phthalates aren't listed anywhere, check again if you will see words such as *time-release, enteric coatings, delayed-release, target-released, and controlled-release.*

Why? Because you do not know what chemical it is that they used for that kind of coatings. Who knows if they used phthalates in it? If you find **even** just one of the words I mentioned above, then do yourself a favor and just opt for a natural remedy or you'll end up spending more than you planned while killing yourself.

- **Phthalates**

What are **phthalates,** anyway? Why are we talking about this chemical? Because your life depends on it, that's why! Before we move on, I would like to tell you about one very important thing:

__The FDA do not require any company to disclose their use of phthalates if they are used in any recipe for drug delivery.__

That means do not expect just about every box or label of medicine to fully declare the ingredients of the drugs they sell. Just because it doesn't say phthalate anywhere doesn't mean it is already safe.

Phthalates is a type of chemical that is used in various type of industrial products and there are also different types of phthalates, just so you know. It is mostly used in plastic products to provide resilience and flexibility. So, why is it used in drugs? Because it helps regulate the release of drugs or those types of drugs that have timed-release.

Now, since we are in the modern age and medicines have also evolved, you will see tons of medicines with plastic coatings. That being said, it only means that there's already lots of common drugs and supplements that contain phthalates. There's still no study about how much phthalates in a pill can cause health problems, but prolonged exposure to this kind of chemical can surely heighten your risk for hormonal, immunological, metabolical, and reproductive problems.

There are many types of phthalates, but the two most common types of this chemical used in drugs are **Dibutyl Phthalate (DBP)** and **Diethyl Phthalate (DEP)**. It was also found by several scientists that there are high levels of broken down phthalate products in the urine of patients who have been taking coated medicines for different types of condition.

- **Drugs and Adverse Reactions**

We all know that every drug has its own adverse reaction. Did you know that studies about the dangers of drugs found out that adverse reactions of drugs, particularly the prescribed ones, is one of the leading causes of illnesses or diseases and death in America? It's the ugly truth.

Numerous prescription for a person isn't exactly helpful either. Some people would think these medications are for maintenance and they shouldn't give it up, but I'd like to cite an example. Say, for example, you are an average senior citizen prescribed with about 5-6 drugs. Here's a fact backed up with studies and research: Prescription drugs disrupt a person's multiple cell functions in order to suppress the symptoms of the disease. Whatever symptom it is that you have in mind, be it a cough, allergies, dizziness, or headache, the drugs given to you are meant to disrupt the cell functions that can cause biochemical changes to *cure* you.

You see, if one drug can cause tons of changes in your body and disrupt multiple cell functions, imagine what 4-6 more drugs taken all together will do. And you are wondering why most of the old people who are

prescribed with tons of medicine are called senile? That's the result of all the medicine they take, it messes up their bodies and mind.

- **Drugs and Side Effects**

Most of the time if you are treating a simple disease like a common cough or colds with some drugs, the side effects that you get are even more harmful than the disease itself. There have been countless instances where a patient died not because of his or her illness, but because of the side effect or the adverse reaction of the drug.

Check the labels before taking any medicines because drug prescription and dosage differ for each and every one of us. Just because one certain drug worked so well for your friend or loved one doesn't mean it will do the same to you.

Drug dosage and prescription depend on your weight, your age, the way your body reacts to certain drugs and chemicals, your current illnesses, and your overall condition. That is the very reason why we have doctors to prescribe us our medications and I am not saying that all doctors prescribe drugs properly. Some of them over-prescribe drugs because of defensive medicine. Always remember, a panacea for one person can be a poison for another.

- **Excessive Intake of Drugs Especially Antibiotics**

In my introduction of this topic, I just mentioned a friend who has an illness right now because of too much intake of paracetamol. If paracetamol can lead your body to suffer from two sessions of dialysis per week, what more can antibiotics do? Have you ever took the time to think of that?

You see, excessive use of any drug can lead to harmful effects. If the result isn't an addiction, they can ruin one, two, or more of your organs especially the kidney that filters just about anything that we put inside our mouths and tummies.

Apart from that, there is also the antibiotics that you have to worry about. You can't abuse the intake of your antibiotics because if you do, you will get to that one point where even the weakest kind of infection cannot be cured anymore no matter what antibiotic you take. That's because each time you take an antibiotic, your body gets a little bit immune to it. Imagine an excessive intake of antibiotic where your body gets highly immune to the antibiotic itself that the poor medicine loses its effect on you.

There is also one last thing I want you to remember. Antibiotics do not only cause immunity after prolonged intakes. Each intake of that type of medicine also destroys your gut flora or the environment of your digestive system. It leads to malnutrition, cellular toxicity, and mal-digestion.

I hope this chapter made you realize very important things that pharmaceutical companies and even some of your doctors wouldn't even dream of divulging.

Chapter 3

Synthetic Medications Versus Natural Medications

Despite everything that's uncovered to you in the last chapter, some of you still want a good side-by-side comparison. Below is a chart for the comparison of both types of medications.

Natural Remedies/Medication		Synthetic/Chemical Medications
Natural remedies and even supplements cost a lot cheaper than medicines sold in pharmacies, may they be over-the-counter or prescribed. Plus, natural remedies do not always involve	Cost	Costs of chemical or synthetic medications are higher than that of the natural remedies and herbal medications. This issue about the cost of chemical synthetic

something that you should take in. It can be exercises and many more, so it is readily available.		medications leave several senior citizens in United States to skip the doses of their medications or even leave the whole prescription unfulfilled.

Mainly, the cause of higher price for synthetic medications are the various chemicals they contain. |
| Natural medications including herbs also include chemicals. While there are arguments about natural supplements, medications, and even herbs that contain chemicals, they are unlike the kind of chemicals that synthetic or chemical medications contain. The only type of chemicals you will find in natural, supplemental, and herbal medicines are | **Chemical Content** | Like I mentioned in the previous chapter that more than half of synthetic medications contain the harmful chemical called *phthalates* that is also used in plastic products and even cigarettes. |

all natural. As for the other types of remedies, well, there's no such thing as deep breathing with chemical content isn't it? It's more friendly to your body.		
There are a few herbs listed with quite an alarming type of side effects like **ephedra** that has been banned in the United States due to reports of high blood pressure and even heart attack from those who have used it. However, these herbs have long been studied and some are even banned. People have been warned about them. As for the other natural medications and remedies, some still have side effects and some do not.	**Side Effects**	There are various side effects for every medicine that belong to this type. Of course, it is only natural to have side effects because chemicals are involve, just like the herbs. The only problem with this type is that, at times, not all the ingredients are listed meaning you do not entirely know what type of chemicals are included in the medicines.
When taken in, it works slowly by letting the normal functions of	**Process**	When taken in, it suppresses disease by disrupting the

the body take place to promote healing.		person's multiple cellular function which messes up your body's biochemistry.

Chapter 4

Organic Remedies

If you are thinking that this book will cover only the organic stuff that can take care of your anxiety levels and symptoms, you are wrong. Yes, it will cover the organic medicines and supplements, but this is only one of the many natural treatments you can use to help keep your anxiety levels checked. Below is a list all for you. I know that some of you are avoiding the sleep-inducing remedies and so, I decided to make things a lot easier for you by labeling the ones that do not induce sleep.

- **Lavender (No Drowse)**

Lavender is known for its relaxing properties, so in case you are feeling extra fidgety or unsettled, a drop of this oil on your collarbone will do the trick. If you have a scheduled big event, make sure to inhale a little bit of lavender oil half an hour before your big event takes place. The good thing about lavender, if you are going to use it as an organic remedy, is that it will never make you feel drowsy.

- **Chamomile**

One cup of chamomile can do just the trick for you if you are suffering from general anxiety disorder (GAD) or even mild anxiety. It has been found that those who are suffering from general anxiety disorder and regularly took chamomile supplements or drank even the tea for eight consecutive weeks resulted into dramatic decrease in symptoms for anxiety. It can easily get rid of the anxiety both from your mind and stomach. However, if you are a very busy person and you want to maintain your productivity, you might as well stay with lavender because chamomile is known for its sleep-inducing qualities.

- **Passion Flower**

The best organic remedy for mild to moderate levels of anxiety. In fact, it can still do lots of good work with severe anxiety. You know why?

Because it helps calm your nerves and that alone helps prevent a lot of anxiety symptoms. The best thing about passion flower is that it doesn't have side effects.

- **Lemon Balm**

Lemon balm has long been known to effectively take care of anxiety and stress. In fact, it is all the more effective once combined with other herbs that can also take care of anxiety or stress, for that matter.

- **Ashwagandha**

Ashwagandha had been in use since the Ayurvedic times to treat those with low energy, stress, and even slow down aging. It has also been known and proven by studies to help with psychological disorders such as Parkinson's disease. It can also lower inflammation. As for anxiety, it helps lower down the sufferer's anxiety levels and even shows dramatic results to those who suffer from agoraphobia or fear of crowded places.

- **Hops**

You can usually find this in beer. However, even before beer, hops has been used and proven to take care of stress, skin disorders, reduce fever, indigestion, lowers uric acid levels, infections, insomnia, and headaches back in the old days. So, if you are taking care of insomnia and stress through hops, imagine how much help it is giving to reduce anxiety symptoms.

- **Green Tea**

Surprise, surprise. To those who are being careful about their diet and saw to it that they regularly drink their green tea, lucky you! You see, you aren't only taking care of your fitness and bowel movement. By drinking green tea, you are also keeping anxiety attack at bay. This is made possible by the amino acid that can be found in green tea and we call it L-theanine. L-theanine helps keep your heart rate and blood pressure regular, keeps your body fit, and reduces anxiety. 5-7 cups a day of green tea will take care of all that worries!

Chapter 5

Let's Talk and Socialize

"What can socializing and talking to people do for my anxiety anyway?" Most likely this question or something along those words is now running in your head. No worries, it is perfectly normal. However, to answer your question and do justice to why I dedicated a whole chapter for this topic, talking, sharing your stories, laughing, and simply keeping the right types of people around you can reduce your stress levels and effectively keep anxiety in its sad corner away from you.

You do not really need a step-by-step instruction for socializing as this habit is deeply embedded in man. It doesn't really matter even if you are an extreme introvert. Remember, no man is an island. That means even the most introvert type of person walking on the face of the planet has that one trusted person or confidant. Even those with *social anxiety disorder.*

If you are one of the few who thinks they haven't found their *confidant* yet, look around you. Chances are, you are simply ignoring the people who genuinely care about you. There is not one person whom nobody cares. It doesn't exactly mean they need to be physically there for you every time, but the moment you came across the words *"one trusted person"* from the previous paragraph, the first person or name that popped in your head is *that person* for you.

You do not need to divulge every little thing to your confidant. Forcing yourself to do so will only give you yet another reason to feel anxious. Go or contact him or her and start some random conversation or the usual topic you two talk about. Listen to what he or she has to say and let them listen to you. Let the words simply flow out of your mind and mouth.

This method may seem close to useless for you, but you will feel a lot better and even cheered up after the conversation. Everything starts small and that is exactly what you are going to do. It doesn't matter how long it will take you until you learn how to function properly in a bigger crowd, as long as you are comfortable with a person or two. That is already a healthy habit that you need to continue doing in order to lower your anxiety levels and keep a trusty friend.

Chapter 6

The Benefits of Exercise in Anxiety

Since common knowledge isn't too hard to acquire now because of the digital age's convenience of putting just about any information right at your fingertips, we now also know how beneficial exercise is for our mental and physical health as it reduces our stress levels.

That being said, stress plays a big role in anxiety disorder like it does with any other disease and disorders. Not to mention inactivity. You know how physically inactive you are as you sit in your office chair, fighting your everyday battles just to bring food to the table, right? This kind of battle also causes you a lot of stress. If you are heavily stressed, chances are you are also suffering from some sort of disease or disorder. Stress eats away at you just like that. Some people even die because of stress alone.

Stress affects the brain and you surely know that the rest of the body is also affected when that happens. Some people perform exercises like aerobics to decrease their stress levels. You see, exercising or any other physical activity can trigger the release of endorphins in our bodies. Endorphins are chemicals that act as our body's natural painkillers and it also helps us sleep better. With that in mind, exercise can cut down your overall tension, fatigue, and stress that have piled up for hours, months, and even years. And guess what, a 5-minute worth of aerobics or a 10-minute walk can already help ward off anxiety disorder. So, now you have more reason to do your exercises regularly.

Wait. How Do Exercise Exactly Work in Anxiety?

Simple. As you burn fats and cut down your inactivity, you are also **burning cortisol.** If you are stressed, fatigued, or burned out, you are most likely to be suffering from anxiety. Now, suffering from anxiety disorder means that your body has high levels of cortisol to the point of excess. If you burn down cortisol as you exercise, it only means that you are also decreasing the levels of your anxiety.

Back when I was still heavily suffering from anxiety disorder and found out what exercise can do for me, I did my best to do exercises whenever I can. Let me share you the tips of what I did to battle my anxiety.

Simple and Really Quick Exercises and Tips

- If you are too busy and can't afford to spare a big block of 20-30 minutes for exercising, make sure that you stand up from your office chair after every 15-20 minutes. Stretch that body as much as you can. Never let your blood and muscles sleep for hours.

- A 10-minute walk can do great wonders when done daily. In fact, as long as you don't stay plastered in your seat for one straight hour can already work wonders. So, walk to the comfort room. Walk to the water dispenser. Walk to the fridge. Do anything that will force you to walk even for short distances.

- Here's one exercise I do daily because I have no excuse not to do it. This will only use **one minute of your precious time** so, there's absolutely no excuse for you as well. Right before you go to the breakfast table or before you go to the shower, perform a one-minute plank. Yes, planking.

- Lie with your stomach on the floor and place your lower arms in front of your chest and flat on the floor as you lift your body and tuck your abdominal muscles. Your lower arms and your toes should be the only parts of your body that will touch the floor. Stay in this position for a minute and do not cheat.

If you are feeling extra generous or it's just the time of the week where you aren't bound to your duties at work, do some yoga, swimming, dancing, relaxed sports, biking, or jogging. That extra oomph of physical activity that you do in the weekend will not only keep you happy and fit. It will also keep anxiety away.

Chapter 7

How Music Affects Your Brain

People say that music touches the soul. It is one of man's surviving hobby that will never, ever go obsolete because man knows subconsciously that music does magic to him. Even children, teens or young adults who do not yet know how to appreciate many things in the world know how to appreciate music. It's true, the young ones' choices and taste in music is quite different, but it changes to better and friendlier tunes as they age.

But, did you also know that music can lower your anxiety and stress levels? Think of music as the brain's version of the exercise. And also keep in mind, anything that lowers your stress levels can help keep you away from high levels of anxiety.

So, going back to music, what it does is just transport you to an entirely different world. If you cannot understand what I am saying, simply close your eyes to heighten all your other senses and listen to music. Your mind's eye will start working and your mind's black screen will start showing you pictures, if not some sort of light travelling in space. 15-20 minutes of relaxing music a day, be it classic, jazz, soft ballads, or instrumentals can reap so much benefits. It can relax you right away. The heart rate changes depending on what you are listening to, so make sure to listen to relaxing ones if you want a healthier and regular heartbeat.

If you haven't tried it, after listening to 15-20 minutes of relaxing music as you close your eyes, try opening them once again as soon as the music has finished. That fresh perspective you experience as soon as you open your eyes isn't something that happened *to your eyes* alone. It also affected you deeper than you think. Music enters the brain, it touches the soul, and even alters how you look at the world.

Let us snap back to the scientific value of music. You see, music is now being used as therapy not only to patients who suffer from anxiety, but also to those who suffer from cancer. That is because it helps relax the patients, help them escape reality even for a couple of minutes and go back to the real world with a more positive outlook in life. Try it if you haven't, because you can never go wrong with music.

Chapter 8

Relaxation Techniques to Battle Anxiety

Finally, here are some techniques that you can do to help you relax whenever you feel a bout of any anxiety symptom. No need for you to worry if anyone's looking or if someone might see, because these techniques are really simple, but they can surely relax you.

1. Slowly breathe in through your nose and fill your lungs with air as much as you can. Slowly exhale through your mouth. Repeat until it calms you and your heartbeat. Remember, your heartbeat says it all. If the beat is irregular, too slow, or too fast, do this relaxation technique to help regulate it.

2. If you are feeling tensed and stressed, pull up your shoulders as close as you can to your ears and then relax them. This works well with the neck and arm stretching.

3. For your neck, simply tilt your head forward until your chin is close to your chest and lift it back to the original position.

4. To rest your tired eyes and lower your stress levels as you sit in your office chair, simply look away from your computer, squint and relax your eyes 3-5 times. Next, bring your brows together and then relax.

5. To promote better blood flow as you sit for long hours in front of your office desk, stretch your arms as far as you can away from your body and relax. Now, flex your hands as you stretch your fingers, then relax. Better yet, mimic how a cat stretches indulgently and you will find it feels better.

6. For your feet and legs, like you did with your arms, simply stretch your legs as far as you can

away from your body and flex your feet then relax.

7. Visualize to help bring some peace to your mind. Go to a quiet place or use your trusty earphones and play a relaxing music as you close your eyes. Let your mind drift to whatever and wherever it wants to go. Remember, never ask yourself questions as you do this, nor try to analyze what is happening because you ruin your mind's drifting as soon as you do. When you are done, don't open your eyes yet and slowly bring your consciousness back. Once you are familiar with the sounds you regularly hear like people walking or talking and doors closing and opening, slowly open your eyes. Do this for 5-10 minutes a day or as much as you like, provided you are in a place where you can sit and relax without someone bothering you.

Conclusion

The battle with anxiety disorder is a continuous one because as long as there is stress, there is always anxiety. Anytime, your anxiety levels can rise higher, especially if left unchecked. That is already a known fact and in case you haven't thought of that yet, condition your mind now with those words.

The good thing about this is that, from now one, every time you think you will soon be battling another wave of an anxiety attack, you know what to do without having to run to your doctor to ask for a piece of paper that can result to ruining your health and cost your life.

Treat anxiety disorder with natural remedies and never be afraid. As long as you can keep those anxiety levels in check, you will do just fine. There's no need for you to chain yourself to maintenance medication and work for the rest of your years just so you can afford them.

Reviews for the book are welcome and if you like it, positive reviews are sure fine ways to keep me going. Thank you again for downloading this book and I hope you learned a lot from it.

CPSIA information can be obtained
at www.ICGtesting.com
Printed in the USA
BVHW042022080819
555432BV00012BA/120/P

9 781532 716416

Marriage:
How to Save and Rebuild Your Connection, Trust, Communication And Intimacy

Peter Jenner

Table of Contents

Introduction

I want to thank you and congratulate you for opening the book, *"Marriage: How to Save and Rebuild Your Connection, Trust, Communication and Intimacy"*.

This book has actionable steps and strategies on how to save your marriage and build trust, communication and intimacy.

"And they lived happily ever after"

That sounds like something out of a fairytale but every couple wishes for 'happily ever afters' when they are tying the knot (except if one or both of them are serious pessimists or sadists). Sadly however, very few couples get to experience this sweet, fairytale kind of marriage. In fact, divorce rates are at an all time high with fifty percent of marriages consummated resulting in divorce or separations.

Don't let anyone fool you; marriage is tough work, and it takes a lot of determination and willpower to sustain it. Imagine having to live with, and deal with the same person for ten years, fifteen years, thirty years or more. Along the line, you might start to feel more like siblings rather than lovers. Your problems may became as simple as a loss of spark in the relationship where you were once madly in love and suddenly do not feel as crazy in love as you used to be. Then it spirals into other relationship problems like lack of intimacy, lack of connection and lack of trust.

If left unchecked, the couple drifts far away from each other and the relationship is damaged and before you know it, you are headed for divorce. The good news is that your marriage doesn't have to feel like a prison sentence. You can enjoy your marriage.

This book will help you do just that by looking at how to bring back the spark, fun, trust and intimacy back into your marriage.

Thanks again for opening this book, I hope you enjoy it!

Chapter 1: The Cold Hard Truth about Marriage

Marriage was never designed to be a bed of roses...............No, it wasn't.

There is no single marriage out there without its own challenges. Forget about your friends who have been telling you about how their marriage is the 'truth' and how they've never had a misunderstanding with their spouse. Forget about those couples you see holding hands and publicly displaying affection all the time. Forget about those movies you've seen where some couple got married and lived happily ever after. That's hardly what happens in the real world.

If you observe any relationship, friendship, or marriage deeply, you would discover that there are always issues and that's because of the human nature.

Humans are naturally different and unique in their needs, desires, wants and tastes. No matter how much two people love each other, they can't always be on the same page all the time. There would be times when one partner sees things a different way or desires a different thing and this is the reason for challenges in marriage.

However, the happiest couples are those who have learnt how to manage the issues in their marriage and keep it from spiraling out of control.

When you started reading this book and you saw this chapter 'the cold hard truth about marriage', I bet you were curious and probably wondering "what's the cold hard truth about marriage?"

Well, the truth about marriage is that there would always be challenges. Notice I didn't call them problems? I called them challenges. They are challenges and not problems because when handled the right way, they can help you to grow even closer and deeper in love. It is when you fail to handle the challenges properly that it becomes a problem.

Life itself is full of challenges. Growing up is a challenge, making money is a challenge, even staying alive is a challenge because you have to make conscious efforts to eat healthy, avoid danger, exercise and ensure that you are nursed back to good health when you fall sick. If you fail to do all of these, you sure wouldn't be too far from the grave.

So don't feel bad, terrible or hopeless when you experience marital challenges. A lady once told me how she felt like a failure because of the problems she was having in her marriage and I know so many men and women who feel this way. But that's just punishing yourself unnecessarily for something that is 'inherent'

It's just like punishing yourself because there was a storm or because the weather is too cold. You have no control over the storm or the weather because they are natural phenomena; they will happen whether you want them to or not.

This same thing goes for marriage. The challenges are inherent. No matter how much you try to play the angel, there would still be challenges. For instance, you decide to agree with anything your partner says just to avoid arguments or misunderstandings. Do you know that even that is dangerous because it could lead to emotional abuse and that in itself is a problem?

Therefore, you cannot run away from challenges in marriage.

Lack of intimacy, communication, or trust in your marriage is not a problem; it is a challenge, a test of how strong your marriage is and you can use the situation in your favor and turn things around to create an even stronger bond in your marriage.

So stop moaning and whining about the challenges in your marriage. Get up, deal with them, and turn the situation around.

The first thing you need to do to rebuild your marriage is learn how to communicate because this is the backbone of every marriage. Therefore, let us look at how to improve your communication to save your marriage.

Chapter 2: Don't Hate, Communicate- How To Improve Communication With Your Partner

Communication meltdown is killing many marriages out there. Instead of people communicating their feelings with their spouse, some couples choose not to communicate at all or use wrong methods of communication such as:

1. Yelling: Some couples choose to yell at their spouse as a way to express anger and dissatisfaction. Rather than cause relief, this further compounds the problem.

2. Competitive Communication: Some other couples see communication as a battle that they must win. They refuse to see it as a way to foster peace or to bring about change. They communicate with their spouse hoping to be the one to win the conversation and this compounds problems.

3. Selfish Communication: Another wrong method of communication that couples adopt today is the selfish form of conversation where one partner makes it about them, forgetting about the needs and desires of the other party. They don't listen or consider the other person's point of view; it's always me, me and me. So how can you improve communication in your marriage?

How To Improve Communication In Your Marriage

If you've been engaging in any of the following harmful communication methods or you have discovered that there is a communication meltdown in your marriage, here are some steps to take to rebuild the communication in your marriage and start communicating the right way:

Become Friends Again: It's easy to communicate with a friend. If your spouse is your best friend, then you would find it easy to communicate with them as a friend rather than as a competitor. Therefore, the first step to take is to rebuild the friendship between you and your spouse and then you can now start thinking about how to rebuild communication.

Rebuild Your Trust: Trust is also very important. Proper communication cannot happen when there is a lack of trust.

Control Your Emotions: You must control your anger, frustrations, and sadness when you are trying to communicate with your partner. Don't let your anger get in the way by resorting to yelling, cussing out and other damaging communication methods. Communication must be seen as a time for repair and restoration and must be approached that way.

Focus on the Positives: Realize that your partner is only human and bound to make mistakes hence you should avoid focusing on the negatives or the things they have done or didn't do.

Censor Your Words: You must be careful with the words that you use. Censor your words and avoid using derogatory or negative words. Before you use any words on your partner, consider how it would feel if the tables were turned and you are the one at the receiving end. If it wouldn't feel pleasant to you, avoid using such words completely.

Lay Good Examples: Lastly, you must always set good communication examples for your partner to follow. Sometimes, your partner might be the bad communicator. Ensure that you adopt good communication methods and continue to make them see the reason for an improvement in how they communicate.

It is important to understand that communication is the backbone of any marriage. If you can communicate effectively then you can easily solve any challenge and problem that you will ever face.

With that in mind, let us now look at how you can reignite the spark in your relationship.

Chapter 3: Where Did The Spark Go? How To Rebuild Connection With Your Partner

In order to improve your marriage, you first must realize where the spark went. When you were courting your partner, you went out on dates, called each other several times a day, sent texts and nothing could keep you away from each other.

Now things seem to have changed. You don't feel those 'butterflies' anymore when you think about your partner, sex has become a chore rather than the romantic, mind blowing experience it used to be and the worst thing is that you have tried so hard to reconnect with your partner but it's just not happening and it seems like it's the end of the road.

What if I told you that more than 90% of couples go through such times in their marriages when it feels like they have grown apart and the spark has faded from their relationship and researchers have discovered that 30-60% of married individuals who cheat on their spouse do so because of the loss of excitement in their relationships.

Rather than cheat on your spouse or run into the arms of someone else, why not try to understand why the affection you feel for your spouse has waned and try to understand what you can do to rebuild this connection. Let us look at things that can lead to a loss of spark in a relationship.

Dishonesty: True love and intimacy is about sharing everything with your partner. It is about allowing yourselves to penetrate each other. Holding things back from your partner is the first thing that causes a loss of connection in your relationship.

The thought of sharing everything with your partner may be scary but throwing all your cards on the table and letting your partner see the real you helps you to connect at a deeper level. You would feel like you know each other well and you can trust each other and that helps you to stay connected to each other.

Poor Sexual Life: You can't rule out the power of sex in any relationship. Sexual energy is very strong and is like glue that cements your marriage. If you and your partner have grown sexually distant, then there is bound to be a loss of connection in your marriage. You wouldn't feel that warmth and affection that was once there and you would become like buddies rather than a couple.

Physical Distance: Too much physical distance can also lead to emotional disconnection in a marriage. For your marriage to continue to grow and thrive there is a need for you to spend time together. When you become too busy with work and other things such that you barely have time to go on dates, talk to each other, and spend time together, it creates a wide emotional gap between you.

Lack of Space: A wise person once said, "marriage is not a prison sentence" but unfortunately today, so many couples treat marriage like a prison sentence. They bring on the "you are married to me now so I own you, I have to know what you are doing, where you are and who you are with at every time of the day"

This kills the connection in your relationship. For a marriage to continue to thrive, there is a need for space and time apart. When you spend too much time together and you are literally in each other's businesses at every point in time, it makes you less attractive to each other. The human brain is designed to desire what it cannot get. When you give your partner the space and opportunity to miss you, it revitalizes your relationship. Just as it is important to spend quality time together, it is also essential to spend time apart; you must create a balance.

Misconceptions: The spark in some marriages also dies because one or both partners have decided to believe in common misconceptions about marriage and relationships. People tell you that after the first two years of your marriage, there's a biochemical drop-off that causes a loss of connection in your relationship. They tell you that it's normal and that there is nothing you can do to stop it from happening and then you believe them and stop bothering to work on your relationship.

Lack of Change: No one likes to have the same food or wear the same dress for years and years; this is too boring and tiring. As humans, we love variety.

When you refuse to grow and change, your partner would certainly get tired of you and there would be a loss of spark in your relationship. You have to continue to look for ways to spice things up. You can't change who you are but you can make continuous improvements that would bring an air of freshness into your relationship. Develop yourself, learn new things about yourselves, and get to know your partner on a different level every day.

There are a million and one ways why couples grow apart and lose the connection in their marriage but these are the most common ones. The good thing is that no matter how bad things may seem to have gotten, you can still rebuild the connection and spark in your marriage and become as crazy as you were for each other in the beginning.

To rebuild the connection in your marriage, here are some steps to take:

Relax: The natural human response to unfavorable situations is to either "fight or flee". This is why the first step to take to rebuild emotional connection in your marriage is to take a deep breath and relax.

Drop the Garbage: Next, you have to drop all the resentment, anger, and frustration. If you're going to repair the connection, then you have to drop the excess weight you are carrying. Forget about what your partner has done or didn't do, all of that doesn't matter anymore. What matters now is the future that you hold together and how to make that future a better one.

Figure out What The Problem is: I have listed a number of reasons why emotional disconnections in marriages occur but every marriage is unique. Therefore, it is up to you to find out the reason for the emotional disconnection in your own marriage. Perhaps you are not spending too much time together, or maybe there is a lack of communication in your marriage. Figure out what it is and only then can you start to rebuild and repair the relationship.

Talk to Your Partner about It: It takes two to tango. If your partner is not in this with you, it would hardly work. You have to bring your partner in on this and make them see the problem. Talk to each about the problem and make joint, conscious decisions to fix it.

Take it Slow: You cannot fix your marriage in one day. Just as you didn't fall in love with your partner in one day, you can't expect to rebuild your emotional connection in one day. You have to take things slow and steady because attempts to force things to happen in one day would only jeopardize your efforts. It is also important to exercise patience, as a small change is better than no change at all.

Let Go of the Negative Behavior: It's not uncommon for couples to develop some negative behaviors to help them cope with the emotional disconnection in their marriages. For instance, one partner might decide to start cheating on the other in order to cope with sexual disconnection in their relationship. Some other partners might take to lying, keeping distance, and not communicating with their partners.

Some of the negative behaviors might be subtle and not as extreme as cheating but they still do damage the relationship. Therefore, you have to let these behaviors go and replace them with positive behaviors. If you've been lying, become honest. If you've been cheating, stop it and start being faithful to your spouse.

Focus on the Positive Qualities: What are those things that you fell in love with when you first met? Make a list of those positive qualities you admired in your partner and start focusing on them rather than on the negative qualities because it is very easy to focus so much on the negative and forget about all the good things about your partner.

Introduce New Things: Get out of the normal routine and introduce some fun in your relationship. Try something fun and exciting, something that would blow your minds away.

Start Touching Each Other: Don't wait until it's time for sex to start touching each other physically. Touch boasts the body's feel-good hormones and promotes affection between people so kiss, touch and hold your partner from time to time and don't just wait to do it in the bedroom.

Give Appreciation: Nothing fosters deep connection more than deep appreciation. Take note of the things your partner does and appreciate them directly for it. Speak out your appreciation and let them know that you appreciate them.

Go on Dates: Give yourselves something to look forward to by planning and going on dates. Dates are not just for when you're still courting; no matter how long you have been married, you must never stop going on romantic dates as this is what keeps the fire burning.

Talk: It's time to stop the guesswork and attempts to read your partner's mind. It's time to start being open and honest and asking your partner questions to know what he or she expects from you and you should also do the same. Conversations don't have to be serious and you don't have to nag. Simple, light-hearted conversations from time to time would help you connect, encourage honesty, and bring deeper connection between you two.

Focus on Yourself: Your relationship with your partner cannot thrive if you don't love yourself. You have to take care of your own individual needs and do the things that you are passionate about and only then would you become interesting to your partner. When you are too predictable and boring, it affects your relationship because there are no surprises, thrills or anything to look forward to. Love yourself, enjoy your life, share it with your partner and watch your relationship thrive.

Chapter 4: The Trust Factor- How To Rebuild Trust In Your Marriage

Betrayal hurts and it hurts very much. When you trust a person not to hurt you because you know that you wouldn't do anything to hurt them either and you could always vouch for them, only to discover at some point that they had betrayed that trust, it hurts. Many people today are in relationships where trust has been broken either due to a partner having an affair or lying about something or maybe not delivering on a promise. All of these situations can slowly damage the level of trust in any relationship.

However, trust is a very important factor in any relationship. A marriage cannot thrive when there is a lack of trust. Trust breeds love and commitment in your marriage and when the trust is broken, it becomes extremely difficult for a couple to share real love.

The good thing is that trust can be rebuilt. It's not just going to happen overnight and it would take a lot of determination and willingness on the part of both partners but slowly and gradually, broken trust can be rebuilt.

Rebuilding of trust in a marriage is a two way street. The offending party can take steps to rebuild the trust and so can the offended.

If you are the offending party, here are some steps you can take to rebuild the trust in your relationship:

1. **Come Clean**: Don't continue to deny or lie about what you have done. It is important to come out completely clean and be honest with your partner about what you have done. Yes, the truth always hurts and may even compound the pain but it's a

healing process; at the end of the day, it would help to rebuild the trust and is way better than continuing to lie about it and leaving your partner to find out more details on his or her own.

2. **Drop the defense**: Being defensive also compounds the problem. To help your partner trust you again, you must show a genuine attempt to work out the issues. You must accept that you are wrong (regardless of whether your partner contributed to making you do it or not) and show genuine repentance.

3. **Discuss Your Reasons for Doing It**: Opening up about your struggles and what motivated your actions can help to prevent further occurrence. If there is anything your partner did or didn't do that inspired your actions, this is the time to talk about it.

4. **Be an Open Book**: Yes, you are entitled to your privacy but if you are really serious about rebuilding the trust in your relationship, you have to become an open book at this point. You have to let your partner in on all aspects of your life; unlock your cell phones, share your email password, and make sure you are always true to your words. This would help your partner to start trusting you again.

When you are the offended and your partner has betrayed your trust, it is difficult to start trusting them again but you can't enjoy your relationship when you don't trust your partner so you must make efforts to start trusting your partner again. Before you can start rebuilding trust, it is important to determine whether it is safe to trust your partner again. You don't want to be hurt a second time so it's important to first know if it's safe to start trusting your partner again before you make any effort to do so. Below are things you can use to determine whether it is safe to trust again:

- Open Communication: Has your partner become more open and willing to communicate more about their feelings and actions?

- Transparency: Has your partner become more transparent? Do they now give you free access to their phone, emails, and any other private accounts? When an offending partner becomes more open and transparent, it shows a genuine willingness to change and shows that they are willing to repair the damage in their relationship.

- Improvement: Look out for signs of improvement. Is your partner showing any signs that they have changed or they are changing?

Look out for these three signs and when you are sure that your partner has truly and genuinely repented, you can now start doing the following to repair your damaged relationship:

1. **Communicate**: The first step towards learning to trust your partner again is communication. You must have a genuine, open conversation with your partner about what has happened and your feelings. Be as open as possible about how you feel about the betrayal. Don't hold anything back because talking is actually therapeutic and you can start all over again on the right footing.

2. **Get on a Team With Your Partner**: For this to work, you both have to be on the same team. Both of you have to be ready to work together to make this happen. If your partner is trying to gain your trust again, you have to help them to make it happen.

3. **Forget about the past, stay in the present:** Don't keep bringing up the past; it's not going to help. You must fight the temptation to continue bringing up your partners past mistakes whenever any issue arises. Forgive your partner and make efforts to drop the baggage and let the past go. Remember that your partner is only human and humans are bound to make mistakes. The only thing that matters now is that they are willing to genuinely repent and work on the relationship.

4. **Set Standards**: To prevent the same thing from happening again in the future, you should set rules and standards and discuss them with your partner. Let them know what you can and cannot do, what you would tolerate and wouldn't. Let your partner know that there would be consequences for certain actions in the future. This would help your partner avoid doing the same thing in the future.

Rebuilding the broken trust in a relationship is something that takes time so don't rush it; give it time.

As much as trust is important in a relationship, intimacy is too. Therefore, we will look at rebuilding intimacy in your marriage in the next chapter.

Chapter 5: Bringing Back The Fun- How To Rebuild Intimacy In Your Marriage

You would be extremely surprised at the number of couples living in a marriage devoid of intimacy today. According to researchers, about 25% of today couples live in a sexless marriage. So if your marriage is lacking intimacy at the moment, you are not alone. However, just as your marriage needs trust, love, and honesty to thrive, it also needs intimacy. Intimacy is very important in every marriage. You cannot afford to allow your sex life to go boring; you become roommates instead of a couple in a marriage. Lack of intimacy in your marriage can also lead to frustration and bring in other problems into your relationship. On the other hand, it's very difficult to maintain the same level of closeness you had with your partner as when you were newly married because after all these years, the kids, the challenges and every other thing in between, it's easy to lose the intimacy.

To repair the intimacy in your marriage, here are some things that you can do:

Understand the Differences in Gender: The intimate needs of a man would always differ from those of a woman and it is very important for you to understand this. You must understand and respect the fact that you and your partner have different sexual needs. If your husband is demanding 'too much sex' you must understand that it is in his nature to do so because he is a man and would naturally have a higher sex drive.

If your wife does not have the same sexual drive as you, you must also understand that she is a woman and her sexual needs and drives would always differ from yours. It is very important for you and your partner to understand this factor and always be tolerant and patient with each other.

Once you understand that you have different sexual needs, then you can chart the way forward of ensuring that you meet each other's needs.

Identify The Problem: What is the real reason why the intimacy has gone from your relationship? What pressures are on you that have caused you to lose interest in intimacy? Are there any financial problems or other stresses that have caused this lack of intimacy? It is important to find out where the problem lies in order for you to know how to begin to fix it.

Understand Your Partner's Intimacy Style: Apart from the fact that the intimacy needs of each gender differs, every individual also has their own unique intimacy style. Some people are very physical and love to be touched while some other people do not like to be touched. Some people love public display of affection while some other people would just freak out if you tried to kiss them in public. It is therefore important for you to understand your partners unique intimacy style and try to work with it.

Give it Time: One step at a time is what it would take. You cannot rush it or expect it to happen overnight. Rather than taking drastic steps to rebuild the intimacy in your marriage, take small, gradual steps one day at a time.

Share Your Secrets: Little secrets would only build up and lead to bigger problems in the future. True intimacy comes from feeling vulnerable to your partner and that can only happen when you genuinely share your secrets with them.

Increase Physical Contact: The hugs, the goodbye kisses, the holding of hands, and all the subtle touches are very important. You may not get the time to have sex everyday or even hold deep conversations but these little physical contacts daily serves as a constant reminder that you are committed to each other.

Avoid Pornography: In the process of trying to rebuild the intimacy in your marriage, pornography is something that you must let go of and this is why; Pornography creates unrealistic expectations from your partner. It triggers body image problems and fears of betrayal and might drive you and your partner further apart from each other.

Sex: You can't deny the place of sex in any marriage. Sex is very important. It is what makes you a couple. Any two people can live together, have dinner together, or share the bills but it takes two people that truly love each other and are emotionally committed, to still enjoy having great sex after years of marriage.

One of the major reasons why so many couples are in sexless marriages today is because the sex has become boring. Hence, it is important to always spice up your sex life by trying out new things, doing it in new places, and continuing to satisfy each other's unique needs.

Work on Self-Esteem: Body image issues and low self-esteem also kills the intimacy in marriage. When you no longer feel attractive, you would find it difficult to share yourself or your body with someone else. Therefore, you have to work on your body and your self-esteem so that you can feel more open to sharing yourself and your body with your partner.

Conclusion

Challenges in your marriage don't have to lead to divorce. No matter what the challenge is in your marriage, you can always fix it. As I mentioned earlier, challenges should be seen as a 'call out' to work harder on your marriage rather than a time to flee.

Thank you again for taking the time to read this book!

I hope this book was able to help you to know how best you can save your marriage.

The next step is to start by working on improving your communication and the spark you once had for each other.

Preview Of "Self Discipline: How to Build Incredible Self Discipline and Maximize Your Chances of Success"

So many of us feel that we don't have enough discipline to succeed in life. We may look at successful people and think "that will never be me". It doesn't have to be that way. You *can* be disciplined. You *can* be successful.

This book contains proven steps and strategies on how to maximize will power and self-discipline. You will learn the true nature of willpower and how it relates to discipline. Once armed with this knowledge, you will be equipped to start ramping up your efforts and make inroads to success in life. You will learn the difference between strategy and planning, which is foundational to achieving long term goals. But that's not all. You will learn some of the best kept secrets of the highly successful: a series of discipline and productivity hacks that will elevate your success and achievement in life.

Chapter 1
Willpower as a Muscle

Underlying our capacity for self-discipline is the quality of willpower. It is willpower that allows us to engage in activities even when we might not want to. Since most of the things we have to do as adults aren't all that fun, our willpower is constantly being taxed. One common misconception about willpower is that it is some innate quality of a person. Some people are just born with more willpower than others, so the conventional wisdom goes. Fortunately for us, this isn't actually the case.

In fact, willpower is quite similar to our musculature system in some very important respects. Just like lifting weights allows us to become stronger and develop larger muscles, willpower can be developed over time through practice and repetition. It's not all good news, though. The flip side to this is that our willpower can become fatigued. You can only exert so much willpower in a day; eventually you will give in to temptation. Fortunately, exercise science has some answers to this problem as well.

We can use some of the principles from exercise science to help us in our quest to develop more willpower, and therefore more self-discipline. One of the key concepts we will borrow is that of *progression*. This is just a fancy way of saying that you have to do more over time to see continued growth and development. So, you can start to develop willpower by conquering small bad habits. You can stop chewing nails, stop checking Facebook, curtail excessive video gaming, *etc*. As time goes on, you will have to tackle larger tasks to keep developing a stronger will. Some examples might be cleaning up your diet by getting rid of junk foods, or getting ahead at work by gradually working more productive hours. The time span for these changes is weeks and months so don't think you have to do it all overnight. As they say, Rome wasn't built in a day.

Just like with exercise, *consistency* is going to be the key. You won't make much progress in the gym if you go full out for a week, and then take two months off. Likewise for developing willpower and discipline, you are going to have to commit to daily action and sustain that over long stretches of time. The trick to doing this is going to be the capacity to work and persist even when motivation wanes. We will discuss how to do that in a later chapter.

The final concept we are going to borrow from exercise science is that of *recovery*. Professional athletes don't train every single day of the week. No, they have to have some time off during the week to allow their bodies to recover. This prevents injury and allows them to sustain a high level of performance over the course of many years. Similarly, with our quest to develop stronger willpower we will have to utilize some recovery periods.

For example, if you are developing your willpower to eat better foods, then you would incorporate some treat meals into your planning. This serves a few different goals. First, the treat meals serve as a reward. It's only natural that humans are motivated by positive rewards, so we can exploit this facet of our psychology to help out our quest. Second, the treat meals help to alleviate some of the tension caused by the constant delayed gratification. If that tension is allowed to mount over really long periods of time, it can result in a complete blow out. Some people will diet for a couple months straight, make all kind of progress, and then snap and binge on an entire box of donuts. This sets them off the rails, and they quit their diet completely. This is a complete disaster for our goals, so it's better to have some treat meals every now and again to keep the bigger picture in focus.

Oh, and one final word about going off the rails. If you have been working hard at developing willpower and have a moment of weakness, then *don't* go off the rails. It's normal to have lapses in discipline sometimes, just don't let it be the end of your journey. Move on with your life and practice some self-forgiveness. In the end, it won't really matter if you slip up once or twice.

Key Takeaways

- Willpower is like a muscle. It can be strengthened and fatigued.
- To keep growing your willpower, you need to take on bigger challenges.
- Daily and persistent exertion of will yields big improvements in discipline.

You will eventually have to take a break from a life of austerity. Having treats or days off is both productive and recommended.

If you want to check out the rest of "Self Discipline: How to Build Incredible Self Discipline and Maximize your Chances of Success

go to: http://amzn.to/1nsn5vp

If the link does not work for whatever reason you simply search for this title on the Amazon website to find it.

Check Out My Other Books

Below you'll find some of my other popular books that are popular on Amazon and Kindle as well. You can visit my author page on Amazon to see the newest books that I have created. Simply search for Peter Jenner on Amazon and go in to my author page.

Self Discipline: How to Build Incredible Self Discipline and Maximize your Chances of Success

Vegan: 31 Delicious and Easy Recipes – Your Everyday Vegan Cookbook

Speed Reading: A Beginner's Guide for Increasing Your Reading Speed by 300 %

You can search for these titles on the Amazon website to find them.